If found, please return to:

_____
name

_____
cell/email

_____
destination

_____
trip dates

_____
trip companions

_____

_____

_____

_____

Serve Mission Trip Journal by Mellanie Kay Journals © 2019, Revised 2020
All rights reserved. No part of this book may be used or reproduced in any manner whatsoever without written permission except in the case of brief quotations embodied in critical articles and reviews.

Indicate your starting point and then your destination(s) with arrows and/or coloring on the map below

THINGS TO REMEMBER
checklist

- ○
- ○
- ○
- ○
- ○
- ○
- ○
- ○
- ○
- ○
- ○
- ○
- ○
- ○
- ○
- ○
- ○
- ○
- ○
- ○
- ○

ITINERARY

Destination: _____
Arrive: _____
Activities: _____
_____

Lodging: _____
Address: _____
_____

Notes: _____
_____

Destination: _____
Arrive: _____
Activities: _____
_____

Lodging: _____
Address: _____
_____

Notes: _____
_____

ITINERARY

Destination:
Arrive:
Activities:

Lodging:
Address:

Notes:

Destination:
Arrive:
Activities:

Lodging:
Address:

Notes:

ITINERARY

Destination: _____
Arrive: _____
Activities: _____
_____
Lodging: _____
Address: _____
_____
Notes: _____
_____
_____

Destination: _____
Arrive: _____
Activities: _____
_____
Lodging: _____
Address: _____
_____
Notes: _____
_____
_____

ITINERARY

Destination: _____

Arrive: _____

Activities: _____

Lodging: _____

Address: _____

Notes: _____

Destination: _____

Arrive: _____

Activities: _____

Lodging: _____

Address: _____

Notes: _____

BUDGET: _____

ACTUAL EXPENSES

DATE	DESCRIPTION	CASH, ATM, CREDIT	AMOUNT/ CURRENCY

The **LORD YOUR GOD** *will be* **WITH YOU WHEREVER** *you go*

JOSHUA 1:9

JOURNAL

HIGHLIGHT OF THE DAY:

_____
_____
_____
_____
_____
_____
_____
_____
_____
_____
_____
_____
_____
_____
_____
_____

PRAYER REQUESTS:

_____
_____
_____
_____
_____
_____
_____
_____

HIGHLIGHT OF THE DAY:

PRAYER REQUESTS:

HIGHLIGHT OF THE DAY:

PRAYER REQUESTS:

HIGHLIGHT OF THE DAY:

PRAYER REQUESTS:

HIGHLIGHT OF THE DAY:

PRAYER REQUESTS:

HIGHLIGHT OF THE DAY:

PRAYER REQUESTS:

HIGHLIGHT OF THE DAY:

PRAYER REQUESTS:

HIGHLIGHT OF THE DAY:

PRAYER REQUESTS:

HIGHLIGHT OF THE DAY:

PRAYER REQUESTS:

HIGHLIGHT OF THE DAY:

PRAYER REQUESTS:

HIGHLIGHT OF THE DAY:

PRAYER REQUESTS:

HIGHLIGHT OF THE DAY:

PRAYER REQUESTS:

HIGHLIGHT OF THE DAY:

PRAYER REQUESTS:

HIGHLIGHT OF THE DAY:

PRAYER REQUESTS:

HIGHLIGHT OF THE DAY:

_____
_____
_____
_____
_____
_____
_____
_____
_____
_____
_____
_____
_____
_____

PRAYER REQUESTS:

_____
_____
_____
_____
_____
_____
_____

HIGHLIGHT OF THE DAY:

PRAYER REQUESTS:

HIGHLIGHT OF THE DAY:

_____
_____
_____
_____
_____
_____
_____
_____
_____
_____
_____
_____
_____
_____
_____

PRAYER REQUESTS:

_____
_____
_____
_____
_____
_____
_____
_____

HIGHLIGHT OF THE DAY:

PRAYER REQUESTS:

HIGHLIGHT OF THE DAY:

PRAYER REQUESTS:

HIGHLIGHT OF THE DAY:

PRAYER REQUESTS:

HIGHLIGHT OF THE DAY:

_____
_____
_____
_____
_____
_____
_____
_____
_____
_____
_____
_____
_____
_____

PRAYER REQUESTS:

_____
_____
_____
_____
_____
_____
_____
_____

HIGHLIGHT OF THE DAY:

PRAYER REQUESTS:

HIGHLIGHT OF THE DAY:

_____
_____
_____
_____
_____
_____
_____
_____
_____
_____
_____
_____
_____

PRAYER REQUESTS:

_____
_____
_____
_____
_____
_____
_____
_____

HIGHLIGHT OF THE DAY:

PRAYER REQUESTS:

HIGHLIGHT OF THE DAY:

PRAYER REQUESTS:

HIGHLIGHT OF THE DAY:

PRAYER REQUESTS:

HIGHLIGHT OF THE DAY:

PRAYER REQUESTS:

HIGHLIGHT OF THE DAY:

PRAYER REQUESTS:

HIGHLIGHT OF THE DAY:

PRAYER REQUESTS:

HIGHLIGHT OF THE DAY:

PRAYER REQUESTS:

HIGHLIGHT OF THE DAY:

PRAYER REQUESTS:

HIGHLIGHT OF THE DAY:

PRAYER REQUESTS:

HIGHLIGHT OF THE DAY:

PRAYER REQUESTS:

HIGHLIGHT OF THE DAY:

PRAYER REQUESTS:

HIGHLIGHT OF THE DAY:

PRAYER REQUESTS:

HIGHLIGHT OF THE DAY:

PRAYER REQUESTS:

HIGHLIGHT OF THE DAY:

PRAYER REQUESTS:

HIGHLIGHT OF THE DAY:

PRAYER REQUESTS:

HIGHLIGHT OF THE DAY:

PRAYER REQUESTS:

HIGHLIGHT OF THE DAY:

PRAYER REQUESTS:

HIGHLIGHT OF THE DAY:

PRAYER REQUESTS:

HIGHLIGHT OF THE DAY:

PRAYER REQUESTS:

HIGHLIGHT OF THE DAY:

PRAYER REQUESTS:

HIGHLIGHT OF THE DAY:

PRAYER REQUESTS:

HIGHLIGHT OF THE DAY:

PRAYER REQUESTS:

... AND WHAT DOTH THE *Lord* REQUIRE OF THEE, BUT TO DO **JUSTLY** AND TO LOVE **MERCY** AND TO WALK **HUMBLY** *with thy God.*

MICAH 6:8

POST TRIP

THANK YOU NOTE REMINDERS
Thank those who helped to make your trip possible

BEST MEMORY

WORST MEMORY

What did God teach me while I was on this trip?

What did I learn about myself?

OTHER NOTES

AUTOGRAPHS

Made in the USA
Las Vegas, NV
15 May 2025